The Changing Role of the Managing Chaplain at Haverigg Prison

The Changing Role of the Managing Chaplain at Haverigg Prison

A Case Study

GLYNN JONES

RESOURCE *Publications* · Eugene, Oregon

THE CHANGING ROLE OF THE MANAGING CHAPLAIN AT
HAVERIGG PRISON
A Case Study

Resource Publications
An Imprint of Wipf and Stock Publishers
199 W. 8th Ave., Suite 3
Eugene, OR 97401

www.wipfandstock.com

ISBN 13: 978-1-4982-3162-6

Manufactured in the U.S.A.   07/07/2015

ABSTRACT

THIS PAPER IS THE result of ethnographic research carried out by the Managing Chaplain at Haverigg Prison. It is the first work of its type since the re-organization of the Prison Service in 2013 under the heading "Fair and Sustainable." Essentially, it is a case study of the role of the Managing Chaplain at Haverigg, with an evaluation of the changing role of the Prison Chaplain—with particular attention to the Chaplain's role as a Christian leader. Much of the content is concerned with perception, both historical and contemporary. The main body of the work identifies relevant background information alongside other models of leadership. It traces the history of the development and perception of the prison chaplaincy and constructs an understanding of the leadership style currently employed. Issues arising include mission (as it applies in this context), the tension between pluralism and the uniqueness of Christ, the implicit suggestion of syncretism, and the use of religion as an intervention. The conclusion includes recommendations for maintaining the integrity of Christian witness while fully respecting all faiths.

CONTENTS

ACKNOWLEDGMENTS

THIS DISSERTATION WAS MADE possible by the financial generosity of the Prison Service; also that of the Governor, staff, and prisoners of Haverigg Prison, who made made honest and forthright contributions to the research as it developed. Particular mention should be made of Catherine Fell and Dot Jeffcott at the Prison Service College library, as well as Donald Mitchell, librarian at Wales Evangelical School of Theology, for their tireless work in sourcing resources on my behalf. Thanks also go to Becky Flux, administration assistant at Haverigg Prison, for her personal support and encouragement throughout. Above all, an acknowledgment that without the patience and selflessness of my wife of 36 years, Liz, this dissertation would not have reached completion.

Soli Deo Gloria!

Reverend Glynn Jones,
September 2013.

INTRODUCTION

Background

THE RATIONALE BEHIND THE selection of this title is that the role of the Prison Chaplain has changed considerably over the years. With the ongoing re-organization of the Prison Service (and chaplaincy), under the heading of "Fair and Sustainable," further radical change began to take shape from April 1, 2013.[1] Academic monographs and journal articles, from both inside and outside the Prison Service, appear to indicate that there has not been a unanimous or consistent view of the role of Chaplain for over fifty years. However, what is clear, is that the dominant hand of Anglican/Christian "brokerage" has (since the watershed moment in 2001 when the Venerable William Noblett was appointed Chaplain General) been replaced by a multiplicity of "equal-status" spiritual leaders of various religions. The findings of this research, within the boundaries of the title, will be expected to form the basis of further Doctor of Ministry research into how "Fair and Sustainable" has developed (in relation to chaplaincy) over its formative years.

The methods employed to engage with the issues are mixed, and include both quantitative and qualitative. Since the methodology is ethnographic in nature, much of this study is descriptive. Permission is required (and has been obtained) from the National Offender Management Service (NOMS) National Research

---

1. National Offender Management Service, *NOMS Business Priorities*

Committee to undertake research in Haverigg Prison. About 10% of the prisoner population was offered the opportunity to participate. These participants were drawn from across the faith communities, with informed consent. A strategy of transparency and anonymity has been employed, by refraining from noting names or attributing comments to individuals. There has been similar engagement with 10% of the prison staff (using a random selection from staff lists) and 100% of the core Chaplaincy Team.

Since this study has been carried out by an on-site practitioner/researcher (the author *is* the Managing Chaplain at Haverigg Prison), there is open acknowledgment that full objectivity is an unrealistic aspiration. In some measure, parts of this research are subjectively influenced by the author being a full-time employee of the Prison Service since 1977, and over that time working/exercising ministry in nine prisons of varying security, age, and gender categories.

Research Focus

The aim of this work is to study the role of Chaplaincy Manager at Haverigg Prison. It will examine the issues arising from a complex model of leadership (of a multi-faith team) in an environment bound by secular policies. It has been suggested that Christian "pastor" would be a more appropriate term than Christian "leader." However, in this context the Prison Service previously understood that the Chaplain was a "pastor." Now, the person who manages the Chaplaincy Team is a "leader" first and a spiritual representative second. Since April 1, 2013 the official terminology has changed. The person who heads the Chaplaincy Team carries the title of Managing Chaplain, and the role is not restricted to those ordained or authorized by their faith group. Indeed, in some prisons the Managing Chaplain is not a religious person at all, but a brief within the portfolio of a secular functional head—usually a Governor grade. The training that accompanies this new (higher-graded Civil Service) role makes it clear that it is "Manager" first, and "Chaplain" second. Mindful of the change of emphasis, this work researches the subject through the lens of a leader/manager who is also a Christian. The term Christian leader is therefore more appropriate than Christian pastor for the purpose of this work. Also, the Prison Service holds a genuine interest in this area of study (which is why it is partially funding it). It is appropriate, therefore, that terminology is employed that will be readily understood by the organization.

Overall Research Aim and Individual Research Objectives

The overall aim of this study is to trace the history of the perception of the role of the Prison Chaplain, and to examine how the current role is practiced, from a Christian perspective. Progressively developing chapters focus on a number of individual objectives:

a) Identify relevant background information in order to contextualize the setting, geography, and ethos. This includes a summary of the leadership model imposed by the structure, alongside a general overview of church leadership models outside a custodial setting;

b) Trace the history of the development and perception of the prison chaplaincy;

c) Construct an understanding of the current perception of the role of Managing Chaplain at Haverigg by appropriate stakeholders;

d) Explore how staff and prisoners alike relate to the leadership style of the current Managing Chaplain at Haverigg.

Contained within the main chapters will be an examination of the related issues of:

a) Mission, as it applies in this context;

b) The tension between pluralism and the uniqueness of Christ;

c) The implicit suggestion of syncretism;

d) The use of religion as an intervention.

Finally, the conclusion will contain recommendations to maintain the integrity of Christian witness while fully respecting minority faiths.

1

LITERATURE REVIEW

A REVIEW OF RELEVANT literature is contained within the main body of this work. As an overview, however, over fifty monographs, journal articles, government legislation papers, magazine articles, internet publications, and unpublished theses have been identified as contributing to the subject. Not all of these have been used, but the range of material can be grouped under five headings.

Framework Documentation

The Chaplaincy Team at Haverigg is subject to a complex, multistranded, hierarchical, and national system of leadership. Each of these strands contributes to the ultimate working out of the team function, and needs to be viewed both individually and corporately. These set the boundaries and management patterns that shape and influence the working practice of the focus of this work.

The Prisons Act (1952)[1] and Prison Rules (1999)[2] are the overarching legislative documents, supported by Prison Service Instruction 51/2011[3], replacing Prison Service Order 4550, which provides more detailed instructions. These accountability and management systems are driven by NOMS, an agency responsible for all offenders serving sentences, whether in prison or the

1. *Prisons Act.*
2. *Prison Rules.*
3. Ministry of Justice, *Faith and Pastoral Care.*

community. This is a relatively recent introduction. Until 2007 the Prison Service and Probation Service came under the control of the Home Office. However, responsibility for these combined services now rests with the Ministry of Justice (MOJ), acting on delegated authority from the Secretary of State for Justice, who retains ultimate responsibility. It is fundamental to the understanding of what follows in this work not to underestimate the impact that these documents have on the working out of the leadership pattern in question. Contained within these (and their supporting documents) are the prescriptive influences that both enable and restrict actual practice. In summary the parts applicable to this work are;

a) Every prison will employ an ordained Anglican as one of the two key officers of the prison (the other key officer being a Governing Governor).

b) The Governing Governor will directly line-manage the Chaplain, or delegate this responsibility to another functional head.

c) Religious services will only be led by those with "counter-terrorist" security clearance, (this being a higher level of security clearance and required only of Governor ranks and Chaplains).

d) No faith group will be allowed to proselytize.

e) All the "protected characteristics" of the Prison Service diversity policy will be observed.[4]

f) Prisoners will not be visited against their will.

g) Chaplaincy teams will be multi-faith, managed, and led by a Co-ordinating Chaplain, whose relationship with other team members will be one of "first among equals."

---

4. Protected characteristics specifically being: age, disability, gender reassignment, marriage and civil partnership, pregnancy and maternity, race, religion or belief, sexual orientation.

Historical

A breadth of publications traces the perception of the role of the Prison Chaplain over the years. Notably, these range from Elkin's overview of the English penal system in 1957,[5] through to Drew's[6] and Rees's[7] job descriptions of the 1970's, and Noblett's "Faith in the Future."[8]

Contemporary

There are many contemporary contributors to the ongoing debate concerning the changing nature of the role of Prison Chaplain and, in particular, its Anglican leadership, which Beckford and Gilliat describe as "brokerage".[9] Less dismissive are publications by Williams[10] and Burnside.[11]

Leadership

Specifically relevant to the "leadership" question are works by Doyle and Smith,[12] Stanley[13], and Tidball.[14]

5. Elkin, *English Penal System.*
6. Drew, *The Chaplain's Job.*
7. Rees, *The Role of the Chaplain.*
8. Noblett, *Faith in the Future.*
9. Beckford and Gilliat, *Religion in Prison.*
10. Williams, *Ministry in Prison.*
11. Burnside, *Religious Interventions.*
12. Doyle and Smith, *Born and Bred?*
13. Stanley et al, *State of the Art.*
14. Tidball, *Ministry by the Book.*

Mission and Related Issues

Stott's work[15] is the long-accepted classic on Christian mission and, while dated, still speaks directly to the current issues that are exercising the church. Bosch[16] appears to give a good, but more up-to-date insight into the same issues, which Wright treats at a deeper academic level.[17] Parallel to these, and commenting primarily on the issues arising, are Kostenberger,[18] Newbigin,[19] and Parshall.[20]

15. Stott, *Christian Mission.*

16. Bosch, *Transforming Mission.*

17. Wright, *The Mission of God.*

18. Kostenberger, *The Place of Mission.*

19. Newbiggin, *Pluralist Society.*

20. Parshall, *Muslim Evangelism.*

2

BACKGROUND INFORMATION

Haverigg Prison

FORMERLY A ROYAL AIR Force base, Haverigg was converted to a prison in 1967. The layout, however, is still very similar to a military garrison. Prisoners are housed within billets and have the freedom to move around, associate, and commune within their own living areas with a minimum of uniformed Prison Officer supervision. The prison covers a vast area of land and has the structure of a village, in that within its secure border can be found many of the features and equivalents of a typical local town, including:

- Administrative/Government Offices.
- Further Education College.
- Sports Complex.
- "Police" Station (where refractory prisoners are arrested and temporarily relocated).
- Industrial Work Areas (productive work for which the prison bids to win contracts).
- Agricultural Work Areas (reflecting the nature of rural Cumbrian community).
- Residential Living Estates (some of which would, in some circumstances, be known as "sink" estates, and others known for their pride in appearance by the occupying residents).

- Job Centre.

- Library.

- Health Care Centre.

- Church and other places of worship.

In total the prison accommodates 644 category "C" (relatively low security) male, adult prisoners. The Prison Service statement of purpose is:

> to serve the public by keeping in custody those committed by the courts. Our duty is to look after them with humanity and help them lead law-abiding and useful lives in custody and after release.[1]

In order to meet this purpose, Haverigg's very large perimeter is surrounded by a high fence, capped with razor wire. The prison ethos is to display to its prisoners pro-social and normative standards, as well as inculcating a work ethic. It requires them to work for payment (or engage in education/training), participate in reducing-reoffending programs, and to contribute to the governance of their section of the prison—as well as sitting as representatives on various committees.

Leadership Models Imposed by Outside Structures

The framework documentation outlined in the literature review emphasizes the limitations of leadership expression. Particularly relevant to the leadership model employed are the following factors:

a) Every prison will employ an ordained Anglican as one of the two key officers of the prison (the other key officer being a Governing Governor).

b) The Governing Governor will directly line-manage the Chaplain or delegate this responsibility to some other functional head.

1. Ministry of Justice, *About HM Prison Service.*

c) Religious services will only be led by those with counter terrorist security clearance—this being a higher level of security clearance and required only of Governor ranks and Chaplains.

d) No faith group will be allowed to proselytize.

e) All the protected characteristics of the Prison Service diversity policy will be observed.

f) Prisoners will not be visited against their will.

g) Chaplaincy teams will be multi-faith, managed, and led by a Managing Chaplain whose relationship with other team members will be one of "first among equals."

Overview of Church Leadership Models

Acknowledging that various forms of church leadership currently exist, it is appropriate to ask if there is a definitive New Testament pattern, and if one form of church government is more scriptural and/or appropriate to a custodial setting than others. These have to be placed within the confines of the imposed and complex structure previously noted, as well as taken into account when drawing conclusions. Grudem, in a broad sweep across the plethora of options helpfully summarizes:

> The Roman Catholic Church has a worldwide government under the authority of the Pope. Episcopalian churches have bishops with regional authority, and archbishops over them. Presbyterian churches grant regional authority to presbyteries and national authority to general assemblies. On the other hand, Baptist churches and many other independent churches have no formal governing authority beyond the local congregation, and affiliation with denominations is on a voluntary basis. Within local churches, Baptists often have a single pastor with a board of deacons, but some have a board of elders as well. Presbyterians have a board of elders and

Episcopalians have a vestry. Other churches simply have a church board.[2]

Quinn and Wacker argue, from a Roman Catholic perspective, for a monarchical episcopate, a three-tier system based on a hierarchy.[3] However, while functional, and with some merit, this does not fit easily within a New Testament framework, and indeed can be more easily traced back to Ignatius of Antioch (c.AD 35–107) in the second, rather than the first, century. Benjamin Merkle goes further and maintains that a monarchical episcopate is "foreign to New Testament documents."

In developing the opposition to three-tier church leadership, Merkle discloses his view that a two-tier model should prevail, consisting of only two types of leaders, namely, elders/overseers and deacons. He further asserts that these offices should be a plurality because (apart from 1 Tim. 5:9), the term "elder" is never used in the singular.[4] It would seem reasonable to conclude that the New Testament does not conform to the three-tier model but more closely to a two-tier pattern, on the grounds that the terms bishop and elder are synonymous and refer to one and the same office.

Comparison can, and should, be made with secular leadership models that overlap the previous overview of church structures, because the Prison Service is overtly a secular institution. Doyle and Smith review models of classical leadership and identify four main generations of theory[5]:

a) Trait theory asserts that those who exhibit certain qualities (or traits) make exceptional leaders. These traits manifest themselves in people who know what they want and how to achieve it. In church terms, the strategic-mission-planner would possess some of the traits cited: task competence,

---

2. Grudem, *Systematic Theology.*

3. Quinn and Wacker, *Letters to Timothy,* 243ff.

4. Merkle, *The Elder and Overseer,* 160.

5. Doyle and Smith, *Born and Bred?*

intelligence and action-oriented judgment, and the capacity to motivate people.

b) Behavior theory is similar, but differs from focusing on traits (personal qualities) to what leaders *do* – how they behave. Doyle and Smith further subdivide this theory into four main components: those who have a concern for the task, with the emphasis on solid objectives; those who are concerned for people and have their interests at heart while achieving the task; those who can exercise directive leadership and take decisions for others; and those who can also share decision making in an act of participative leadership. Many of these characteristics can be seen in churches that rely predominantly on one leader.

c) Contingency theory places an emphasis on those who are able to react to what is needed in rapidly changing situations and circumstances. Sometimes this is in a time of crisis, as with military leaders in a combat situation. Church leaders who are the focus of media attention for some reason, perhaps a community tragedy or a church scandal, may well come under this heading of being competently able to react to situations as they arise.

d) Transformational theory speaks of the leader who is able to motivate by charisma, by their very personality and presence. The transformational leader is one to whom a member of the team would turn to when in distress or needing direct answers. This can lend itself to an unhealthy, ego-driven focus when applied to church leadership. There is an inherent spiritual danger when the pastor encourages the belief among his flock that the pastor has special gifts, and the solution to the problem lies in *their* discernment alone.

While there are other secular leadership models, for example, sports coach, teacher and military commander, the one most frequently cited is that of the Chief Executive Officer (CEO). There is a suspicion that the world of business and commerce (along with the Prison Service) drives toward a given target sometimes at the expense of its workforce, that the mantra of a successful CEO is "the end justifies the means." These characteristics, while often admired for the results that they produce for the establishment, may not be considered the best driving force for one who seeks to pastor and grow disciples. Much has been written urging against adopting this model, including Piper, who emphatically calls upon Christian leaders to reject worldly models on the basis that Christian leaders are:

> fools for Christ's sake. But professionals are wise. We are weak. But professionals are strong. Professionals are held in honour. We are in disrepute. We do not try to secure a professional lifestyle, but we are ready to hunger and thirst and be ill-clad and homeless.[6]

There are, however, authentic church leaders who do support the concept of a CEO approach to church leadership. One notable exponent of CEO-type leadership is Andy Stanley, pastor of the highly successful Northpoint Community Church in Atlanta, Georgia. In an interview with *Leadership Journal* Stanley expressed his content with being seen as more of a CEO than a pastor. When asked if the church should stop talking about pastors as shepherds, Stanley is reported as saying:

> Absolutely. That word needs to go away. Jesus talked about shepherds because there was one over there in a pasture He could point to . . . it was culturally relevant in the time of Jesus but it's not culturally relevant any more. Nothing works in our culture with that model except this sense of gentle, pastoral care. Obviously that is a facet of church ministry, but that's not leadership.[7]

Carnes quotes the interview further:

> When the interviewer pressed Stanley asking "Isn't shepherd the Biblical word for pastor?" Stanley demurred: "It's the first century word. If Jesus were here today, would He talk about shepherds? No . . . By the time of the book of

6. Piper, *Brothers.*
7. Stanley et al., *State of the Art.*

Acts the shepherd model is gone. It's about establishing elders and deacons and their qualifications. Shepherding doesn't seem to be the emphasis. Even when it was, it was cultural, an illustration of something. What we have to do is identify the principle, which is that the leader is responsible for the care of the people he's been given. That I am to care for and equip the people in the organization to follow Jesus. But when we take the literal illustration and bring it into our culture then people can make it anything they want because nobody knows much about it."[8]

Care has been taken to comprehensively describe the overall structures and working ethos of Haverigg , the legislative protocols it is bound to, and the various models of leadership (both secular and ecclesiastical) that it is influenced by. All of these apparently abstract themes have a direct bearing on the function, practice, and management of the Chaplaincy Team at Haverigg.

8. Carnes, *Like Sheep.*

3

HISTORY OF THE DEVELOPMENT AND PERCEPTION OF THE PRISON CHAPLAIN

THE INTENTION OF THIS chapter is to identify and evaluate the perception of the Prison Chaplain through a "time-line" gathering of significant historical events. In order to view this section in context, some dates are included with no reference to Chaplains. Ancient and modern documents are used as primary sources and, where applicable, these are reviewed.

1553: Bridewell Prison opened as the first "House of Correction" in London. Its purpose was to impose instant punishment on the "disorderly poor." No trial was required and Justices of the Peace (JP) could order immediate imprisonment.

1576: Houses of Correction were seen as a successful means of addressing petty misdemeanors. By **1576**: every county in England had one. By this time they were known colloquially as Bridewells.

1735: Although it is known that hanging had been taking place as a form of punishment at least since the Anglo-Saxon period, the first official records of judicial hanging date back only to 1735. The role of the Chaplain (as a "literate") was to prepare petitions for mercy to the King, and to pray for those who were unsuccessful in their pleas.

1773: Recognizing the centrality of the Chaplain's part in the judicial process, Parliament authorized the appointment and payment of Chaplains to prisons, but withheld from them the authority to demand compulsory attendance.

1775: Prisons began to take a higher profile as a means of punishment. Before this, transportation and hanging were the preferred options for more serious crimes than incarceration in a Bridewell permitted. Prior to 1775, in the absence of more substantial jails, a form of punishment not as extreme as hanging was sought. To this end, transportation was introduced in 1717. Prisoners were removed to the United States until this no longer became a legal option after independence in 1776. Thereafter, prisoners were transported to Australia.

1779: Higher status and authority was conferred upon the Chaplain by a Parliamentary Act, which made provision for compulsory chapel attendance.

1830: In an attempt to draw a closer parallel to the reformation of prisoners with religious penitence, Reverend Daniel Nihil was appointed "Chaplain-Governor" to Millbank prison. Chaplain and Governor in one combined role was chaplaincy profile at its peak. There were, however, some misgivings about the ethos behind this appointment. Scott quotes W.C. Clay from, "Prison Chaplain: A Memoir of the Reverend John Clay," who judges this to be an "unwise project . . . a failure":

> Terrors of the law were abundantly preached in chapel, tracts were diligently circulated in the wards, and the turnkeys transformed into scripture readers and sent on pastoral visits from cell to cell. Of course all the rediest rogues played the game, donned the sanctimonious demeaner, and curried favour by hypocrisy, while a few of the weaker sort went mad under the combined influence of solitude, malaria and Calvinism.[1]

1. Scott, *God's Messengers.*

More recently, Louis Blom-Cooper, speaking at the Tanner Lectures in 1987, explained that the philosopher Jeremy Bentham recognized that all punishment is evil, but that it was justifiable, and possible, to use this evil to induce people to be good. This was the principle enshrined in Millbank, which Reverend Nihil, in his capacity as Chaplain-Governor, was to drive. According to Blom-Cooper, quoting Mayhew and Binney:

> The most successful simulator of holiness became the most favoured prisoner, so that sanctimonious looks were . . . the order of the day, and the most desperate of convicts in the prison found it advantageous to complete their criminal character by the addition of hypocrisy.[2]

1842: Despite the evident failings of Millbank, Pentonville Prison is opened in 1842 based on a model of penitence drawn from solitude, hard labor, and religious indoctrination. Thus, the status and perception of the Chaplain as central to the role of reformation was again enhanced, giving what Scott (quoting Ignatieff) saw as "extraordinary powers over the psyche of the offender."[3]

c1850: The perception of Chaplains as an integral part of the whole system, rather than the spiritual only, is enhanced further when Chaplains are entrusted to perform secular duties. In particular, this involved them taking on the role of Head of Education. By 1922, however, Webb and Webb, in their overview *English Prisons Under Local Government*, contended that education meant:

> little more than the reduction of the prisoner to a state of abject submission supposed to be produced by compelling them to contemplate pictures of eternal suffering to which they were destined.[4]

1863: The "gate-keeping" role of the Anglican Chaplain was causing some considerable unrest. Consequently a new, controversial,

2. Blom-Cooper, *The Penalty of Imprisonment.*
3. Scott, *God's Messengers*, 13.
4. Webb and Webb, *English Prisons*, 158.

Prisons Ministers Act was approved, authorizing the appointment of non-Anglican Chaplains.

1865: Possibly to dampen some of the disquiet following the 1863 Prison Ministers Act, a new Prisons Act reinforced the position of the Anglican Chaplain by stipulating that every prison must "appoint a chaplain, being a clergyman of the established church." As well as allaying fears that the Church of England was being undermined by the appointment of Roman Catholic priests and non-conformist ministers, this removed discretion from local counties concerning chaplaincy appointments.

1877: In order to clarify and introduce consistency of structure to each prison, a new Prison Rule was introduced, naming the Governor, Medical Officer, and Chaplain as "superior officers of the prison."

1896: Since Prisons Acts and Rules had conferred formal responsibilities as well as rights to Chaplains, the Departmental Committee on Prisons recommended that Chaplains should have formal oversight through the appointment of a Chaplain Inspector. G.P. Merrick was duly appointed.

1898: Merrick presented his first chaplaincy report to the Prison Commissioners.

1908: C.B. Simpson was appointed as new Chaplain Inspector. Simpson held this post until his retirement in 1915, making annual reports on the work of chaplaincy to the Prison Commissioners.

1916: After the retirement of Simpson, the Committee on Public Retrenchment recommended that Chaplains' reports were omitted from the published annual Commissioners Report. This recommendation was accepted and acted upon immediately thus, arguably, reducing the profile of Prison Chaplains, nationally and publicly.

1922: Hobhouse and Brockway edited the report, English Prisons Today: Being the Report of the Prison System Enquiry Committee.[5] The report Foreword explains that the official sounding Prison System Enquiry Committee was, in fact, established in 1919 by the Labour Research Department. By 1922 it was felt that a valuable pool of evidence was available from those men and women who had formerly been imprisoned as suffragettes and pacifists and that, since there was little prospect of a government enquiry, this less official investigation would have significant advantages. Some hold that this critique of the whole of the prison system was the forerunner to the challenges of prison reform that continue to this day. Hobhouse and Brockway were drawn from that "pool of valuable evidence" after serving prison sentences themselves. Hobhouse, an "unconditional conscientious objector," refused to do anything to assist the war effort, even serve in the Friends Ambulance Unit. He was sentenced to imprisonment with hard labor and subsequently found himself in solitary confinement for refusing to obey the rule of silence, which forbade prisoners to speak to one another. It was in prison that Hobhouse met Brockway, a socialist and anti-war activist. The final report is a scathing attack on the prison system, and in particular the control the system had over Chaplains. Hobhouse, himself a Christian, noted:

> Under the present system the chaplains are too much under the control of the Commissioners, far too deeply involved in officialdom; that as a rule, they have a great too many duties to perform, too many prisoners to visit, too many forms to fill in too much routine and secular work; and lastly that their Christian work is hampered almost fatally by the repressive thoroughly unchristian character of the system in which they are involved.[6]

1952: New Prisons Act re-stated that every prison must have "a Governor, medical officer and chaplain" (of the Church of England).

5. Hobhouse and Brockway, English Prisons Today.
6. Hobhouse and Brockway, English Prisons Today, 188.

1957: First Principal Roman Catholic Chaplain appointed.

1957: A monograph by Winifred Elkin[7] discussed in detail the claims of the English penal system to be a re-educating force for the law-breaker. Elkin gravitated toward the Howard League for Penal Reform as an administrator, speaker, and writer after beginning her career as an economist. In this work she expresses her interest in a broad sweep of the general treatment of offenders. In particular, she notes the worth of Chaplains at that time and explains that:

> No appointment is made for more than seven years. It is felt that with longer appointments there would be a danger that the Chaplain would lose his freshness and enthusiasm in the specialized and difficult atmosphere of a prison.[8]

In context with the chapter in question, it would appear that Elkin is emphasizing that Chaplains were under pressure, in her view, due to their central position within the system. She also acknowledges that much of their work is not quantifiable when she states: "Their most valuable achievements may be known only to those prisoners whom they have helped."[9]

1963: It appears from sources that, although the 1952 Prisons Act gave a boost to the relative position of the Chaplain, by 1963 there had been a clear down-turn in the perception of their place within the system. Stanley Pearce conducted a review for the Prison Service Journal and noted:

> Today, the Chaplain has a sterner task to face. His status is not automatically guaranteed to him by the structure of the system. He must be prepared to justify his existence, either in competition or in collaboration with those who have relieved him of his extra-spiritual duties.[10]

7. Elkin, *The English Penal System.*
8. Ibid., 167.
9. Ibid., 169.
10. Pearce, *The Chaplain's Place*, 38.

Pearce also notes that, although the Chaplain still holds a statutory position, this does not preserve his historic status as "number three" (after the Governor and Medical Officer) for the issue of prison keys. He observes a lowering of status and offers a possible rationale:

> The chaplains keys are now No.12! This is not a complaint. It is an indication of a trend, a shift of emphasis. It certainly emphasises the challenge. Sentimental theory and hard practice are not necessarily identical in their effects, and I believe that there is a current of opinion within the modern theory of therepeutic [sic] treatment which would see the Chaplain, not so much as essential or necessary, but as a conciliatory concession to the "establishment."[11]

1963: The lowering of chaplaincy status from the Pearce article is, in the same year, further emphasized by Scott, who observes that "If 'Prisons Today' was an indicator of how much academic interest was shown in the Prison Chaplain in the twenties, then conversely the virtual omission of religion in the psychological study 'Pentonville' by Morris and Morris (1963) must gage [sic] how far this appreciation had declined".[12]

1967: The report on the work of the Prison Department for 1967 (presented to Parliament in 1968) contains a chapter on religion.[13] It highlights the growth in numbers of Sikh, Buddhist, and Muslim prisoners and the need for Chaplains to engage in dialogue with non-Christian faith representatives. As a further expansion of the traditional role of the Chaplain it states that "chaplains need to be enabled to explore the possibilities of applying to the moral and religious areas the techniques and methods now used in . . . psychology, psychiatry, social science, and professional counseling."[14]

---

11. Pearce, *The Chaplain's Place*, 41.

12. Scott, *God's Messengers*, 17.

13. Home Office, *Work of the Prison Department*.

14. Ibid., 32.

To this end, an ongoing program of formal training for full-time Chaplains and Roman Catholic priests began in 1967.

c1967: Compulsory attendance at chapel abolished.

1968: Abbott, writing in the Prison Service Journal, takes the view that the profile and status of the Chaplain is in continuing decline and points to, by this time, all Chaplains being allocated key number 12.[15]

1972: Formal Chaplain's Job Analysis drawn up by J.H. Drew, Assistant Chaplain General.[16]

1975: L.L.Rees was the Chaplain General between 1962 and 1980, after which he was elevated to the episcopate. The Prison Service College holds hand-written notes that were made up by him that define the work of chaplaincy under three headings: pastor, priest, and prophet. These notes were subsequently used by Rees in the delivery of a lecture to the Howard League of Penal Reform on June 19, 1975. Rees describes his long association with the Prison Service and the changes in perception of the Chaplain's role he had seen during that time. He points out that he was the Chaplain General who recommended the abolition of compulsory chapel attendance. It had become, as he saw it, "an exercise in dishonesty."[17]

Rees contends that the role of pastor is not unique to the Chaplain, but that it is shared by all others in the prison who have a concern for others. The particular specialism that the Chaplain brings is to discover what God's will is for the prisoner and what part he, as the Chaplain, is to play. He feels that this may be simple friendship because "often a man has to find a friend before he can find God, or be found of Him."[18]

In his priestly role, Rees understands the part of the Chaplain to be the link between the prisoner and God's scheme of

---

15. Abbott, *The Prison Chaplain*, 22.
16. Drew, *The Chaplain's Jobs*.
17. Rees, *The Role of the Chaplain*.
18. Ibid.

redemption. He speaks of the Chaplain as being the man of prayer, dispenser of sacraments, and leader of worship. The Chaplain is the person in the system who moves "within the structure of grace."[19]

Finally, Rees acknowledges that the Chaplain has theological insights that have a bearing on the whole of life, not just the "religious" part. He identifies this as the prophetic. When the Chaplain asks the extra question he is, according to Rees, exercising a prophetic role, which is not entirely unique to the function of a Chaplain, but very much a part of his "accepting the restraint of that position as well as its privilege."[20]

Rees, in attempting to make a definition of the Chaplain's role at that time, acknowledges the difficulty of such a task in an ever fluid situation. His three-fold model of prophetic, priestly, and pastoral is an opportunity to emphasize the distinctiveness of Christian ministry. He does, in my opinion, miss this by enrolling others into at least two of these headings. He says of the pastoral role that: "This of course is a role which is not unique to the Chaplain – it is shared by all others who have a concern for prisoners as people." Of the prophetic nature of chaplaincy, he asserts that:

> He is not the only person with theological insights, with a commitment to the religious doctrine of man. The Christian Church in prison, the Church within the Prison Department is not made up of clergy – it is made up of all Christians whose contribution is rooted in their Christian belief even where this is not publicised.[21]

1997: Scott's research into the contribution of the contemporary Prison Chaplain to the prison community concludes with a chapter entitled "Findings and Evaluation of the Research."[22] This provides a relevant "snapshot" since the last documentation, identifying the perception of the role of the Chaplain some twenty-two years previously. Relevant subsections of the chapter focus on: a)

19. Ibid.
20. Ibid.
21. Ibid.
22. Scott, *God's Messengers*, 40-4.

The Chaplain and the Hierarchy of the Prison; b) The Chaplain and the Prisoners; and c) The Chaplain.

"The Chaplain and the Hierarchy of the Prison" essentially narrates the view that prison staff (particularly Prison Officers) have of Chaplains. In summary, there appears to be considerable mistrust due to misunderstanding of what Chaplains are there to do. Scott's research suggests that the perception of Chaplains by other members of staff depends more on the individual personality of the minister rather than the position of the Chaplain. Thus, according to Scott, "respect is earned rather than ascribed."[23]

"The Chaplain and the Prisoners" attempts to assess how Chaplains are viewed by prisoners. Scott acknowledges that this is difficult, because many act differently when in a group than they do when seeing a Chaplain one-to-one. The pendulum of perception swings between the openly hostile, refusing even to talk to a Chaplain, and those who were genuinely pleased to see a Chaplain for a personal discussion. The deciding factor, Scott suggests, is the state of "normality" of the individual. When prison life was "normal" for a prisoner, he saw the Chaplain as just another key-carrying (authority-wielding?) member of staff. When there were difficulties in a prisoner's life, however, the Chaplain was seen as a welcome, supportive resource, distinct from other staff members.

"The Chaplain" section of the findings and evaluation chapter captures the view that Chaplains have of themselves. In summary, this is all positive and tied up in spiritual and pastoral provision. None of the fears of Hobhouse or Pearce are expressed. None mention an imbalance between clerical and secular expectations. None report that (lack of) status is a hindrance to their work and ministry. The overwhelming view expressed is that "Chaplains view their role as a counselor to both prisoner and staff. Chaplains are therefore in a unique position, and cannot be compared to any other member of staff." [24]

Scott's work is a pivotal document in understanding some of the subtleties of change in the history of the perception of the

23. Ibid., 41.
24. Ibid., 43.

role of the Chaplain. His work does, however, disclose his own uneasiness with the link between church, state, and punishment. Indeed, he expresses implicit disappointment that Chaplains "do not contest the appropriateness of the prison as a form of punishment . . . Chaplains could play a crucial role in the reform/abolition of prisons."[25] As Professor of Criminology at the University of Central Lancashire (UCLAN), David Scott continues to promote the cause of the abolition of prisons.

2003: In "Ministry in Prison: Theological Reflections," former Archbishop of Canterbury, Rowan Williams, revisits chaplaincy in prisons and challenges the prophetic, priest, and pastoral model offered by Rees some twenty-eight years previously.[26] The source of this article is an original address to Prison Chaplains in 1994, when Williams was Bishop of Monmouth. He contends that if a distinction is forced between pastoral and prophetic ministry, there is a natural inclination to put prison chaplaincy on the non-prophetic side. Williams also views the pastoral ministry as emanating from Jesus' description of himself in the fourth gospel as a shepherd of his people. He takes the position that the primary image here is about nurture and feeding. Rees contends that these are not unique to the Chaplain, and I suspect that Williams would not disagree. Where Williams does differ, however, is that the pastor/shepherd runs a risk to his own life or identity. He would argue this is not shared with other agencies or individuals within the system.

2008: William Noblett, Chaplain General, writing in the Prison Service News, announces the impending arrival of a "Faith-Awareness Training Package," a three-hour module presented by Chaplains.[27] This training is mandatory for prison staff of all ranks and grades. Its presentation by Chaplains is a significant raising of the chaplaincy profile, both nationally and locally.

25. Ibid., 43.
26. Williams, *Ministry in Prison*.
27. Noblett, *Faith in the Future*.

2011: The post of Principal Roman Catholic Chaplain is removed and replaced with an advisor from outside the Prison Service. Roman Catholic Bishop Brain, President of the Roman Catholic Bishops' Conference, had written to all Roman Catholic Chaplains and Bishops outlining a proposal to utilize an "advisor" to the Prison Service from outside NOMS. This advisor would be answerable to the Bishop's Conference, not to NOMS. Monsignor Malachy Keegan held the post at the time of the proposal. It had been agreed that he would leave the employ of the Prison Service with an attractive "voluntary early departure" package. This caused much consternation among Roman Catholic Prison Chaplains. A large body of them appended their signatures to a letter addressed to Roman Catholic Archbishop Nichols during Low Week of 2011 stating:

> We write to you to express our deep concern and anxiety . . . we have not in any way been consulted . . . there has been a complete lack of transparency and we have yet to have a promised meeting . . . this move will be viewed with suspicion by many Governing Governors . . . a large number of Chaplains do not have confidence in Mgr Keegan and are concerned in the way his new appointment as the 'Catholic Bishops' Prisons Advisor' has been simply presented to us as a fait accompli. We are also aware that Fr Malachy did not "resign his position." He took advantage of the voluntary early departure scheme . . . we believe it to be detrimental and harmful to our work and positions as Catholic prison chaplains.[28]

2011: Andrew Todd and Lee Tipton completed their research for Cardiff Centre for Chaplaincy Studies on behalf of NOMS.[29] This is the most up-to-date pre-"Fair and Sustainable" report. It investigates the role and contribution of a multi-faith prison chaplaincy to the contemporary Prison Service. It acknowledges that "the role of the Prison Chaplain has changed, and continues to change in response to the socio-cultural, political and economic

28. Roman Catholic Prison Chaplains, *Archbishop Nichols*.
29. Todd and Tipton, *Multi-Faith Prison Chaplaincy*.

climate it operates within."[30] When the research was carried out, in 2010, Todd and Tipton could not have foreseen the further major change that chaplaincy would be subject to under the (at that time) unannounced "Fair and Sustainable" re-organization of the Prison Service. They observed that the value of chaplaincy was its "otherness." Their conclusion was that Chaplains were particularly distinctive from Prison Officers and that they provided a place that was "safe." All this, they contend, shapes the current perception of the Chaplain because it, "contributes to a sense, particularly from Prison Officers and Governors, that Chaplains have something of a "neutral", or "independent," status within the prison."[31] The outworking of "Fair and Sustainable" may well bring into question this neutrality.

2012: The Venerable William Noblett, CBE, retired as Chaplain General.

2013: Following some delay, due to discussions about whether Noblett's replacement would be another Anglican or a Free Church minister, or even someone from a non-Christian faith group, Reverend Mike Kavanagh (Anglican), was appointed to the post of Chaplain General.

2013: Implementation of Prison Service re-organization under the heading of "Fair and Sustainable." Effective from April 1, 2013 those Chaplains who were previously known as "co-ordinators" could now opt to remain at "band 5" without any line-management or co-ordinating duties, or apply for promotion to the newly created "band 7— Managing Chaplain" post. The band 7 grade is a senior manager within the establishment, parallel to other Governors as well as non-operational senior staff. On the surface, this may be seen as a clear raising of the profile and status of the Chaplain. However, with the emphasis on "Manager" before "Chaplain," some Governing Governors opted to fill this post with a non-ordained, secular manager—this on the grounds

30. Ibid., 3.
31. Ibid., 5.

that chaplaincy is simply another resource that has to be managed, and can justifiably be included within a wider portfolio that does not necessarily (or advantageously) need a "minister" to fill. At the time of writing, it is not clear how this has changed the perception of the Chaplain in the eyes of staff and prisoners. The surveys and focus groups supporting this study reflect only a little understanding of the changes that have yet to make a substantial impact. They mostly appear to draw on an understanding of chaplaincy prior to "Fair and Sustainable."

4

PERCEPTION OF THE ROLE OF THE MANAGING CHAPLAIN AT HAVERIGG PRISON

Findings From General Staff

The global e-mail list for Haverigg Prison contains the internal contact details for all employed and contracted staff. At the time of research it contained 340 entries. Thirty-four (10% of total staff) were randomly (every tenth name on list) selected to receive a survey questionnaire, along with a participation consent form. Seventeen staff responded, representing 5% of the total staff at that time.

The survey, in the form of a Likert scale, asked participants to indicate, on a tick-box, their responses to the following statements, as well as expressing an opinion as to the three most and least important tasks for the Managing Chaplain;

1. The Managing Chaplain at Haverigg Prison should be a member of the Senior Management Team.

17.6% (3) strongly agreed.

23.5% (4) agreed.

47% (8) expressed no strong opinion.

11.7 (2) disagreed.

0 strongly disagreed.

11.7% (2) viewed membership of the Senior Management Team (SMT) as one of the most important tasks of the Managing Chaplain.

35.2% (6) viewed membership of the SMT as one of the least important tasks of the Managing Chaplain.

2. The current Managing Chaplain should conduct and lead services of Christian worship.

11.7% (2) strongly agreed.

88.2% (15) agreed.

0 expressed no strong opinion.

0 disagreed.

0 strongly disagreed.

35.2% (6) expressed a view that the conducting and leading of Christian worship are among the most important tasks of the Managing Chaplain.

11.7% (2) returned an opinion that the leading and conducting of Christian worship are among the least important tasks of the Managing Chaplain.

3. The current Managing Chaplain should co-ordinate and organize worship for non-Christians.

0 Strongly agreed.

47.0% (8) agreed.

29.4% (5) expressed no strong opinion.

23.5% (4) disagreed.

0 strongly disagreed.

11.7% (2) responded that the co-ordinating and organizing of worship for non-Christians is among the most important of the Managing Chaplain's duties.

17.6% (3) regarded the co-ordinating and organizing of worship for non-Christians as among the least important duties of the Managing Chaplain.

4. The current Managing Chaplain should make Jesus known to all.

0% strongly agreed.

11.7% (2) agreed.

47% (8) expressed no strong opinion.

11.7% (2) disagreed.

11.7% (2) strongly disagreed.

17.6% (3) did not tick any of the available boxes.

17.6% (3) expressed that making Jesus known to all is among the most important of the Managing Chaplain's tasks.

23.5% (4) responded that making Jesus known to all is among the least of the Managing Chaplain's tasks.

5. The current Managing Chaplain should be invited to (and attend) key operational and policy meetings within the prison.

41.1% (7) strongly agreed.

58.8% (8) agreed.

0 expressed no strong opinion.

0 disagreed.

0 strongly disagreed.

29.5% (5) viewed the invitation and attendance at key operational and policy meetings among the most important of the Managing Chaplain's tasks.

11.7% (2) viewed the invitation and attendance at key operational and policy meetings among the least important of the Managing Chaplain's tasks.

6. The current Managing Chaplain should seek to make Christian disciples.

0 strongly agreed.

0 agreed.

64.7% (11) expressed no strong opinion.

35.2% (6) disagreed.

0 strongly disagreed.

0 responded that one of the Managing Chaplain's most important tasks is to seek to make disciples.

47.7% (8) responded that one of the Managing Chaplain's least important tasks is to seek to make disciples.

7.The current Managing Chaplain should proactively represent the prison favorably to the public.

29.4% (5) strongly agreed.

58.8% (10) agreed.

0 expressed no strong opinion.

11.7% (5) disagreed.

0 strongly disagreed.

17.6% (3) returned that proactively representing the prison favorably to the public is one of the Managing Chaplain's most important tasks.

5.8% (1) returned that proactively representing the prison favorably to the public is one of the Managing Chaplain's least important tasks.

8. The current Managing Chaplain should champion non-Christian faith interests.

17.6% (3) strongly agreed.

35.2% (6) agreed.

41.1% (7) expressed no strong opinion.

5.8% (1) disagreed.

0 strongly disagreed.

0 viewed the championing of non-Christian faith interests as one of the most important duties of the Managing Chaplain.

5.8% (1) viewed the championing of non-Christian faith interests as one of the least important duties of the Managing Chaplain.

9. The current Managing Chaplain should promote all faiths.

11.7% (2) strongly agreed.

76.4% (13) agreed.

5.8% (1) expressed no strong opinion.

5.8% (1) disagreed.

0 strongly disagreed.

11.7% (2) expressed the view that the promotion of all faiths by the Managing Chaplain is one of his most important tasks.

0 expressed the view that the promotion of all faiths by the Managing Chaplain is one of his least important tasks.

10. The current Managing Chaplain should contribute to, and be line-managed by, the Reducing Re-Offending group.

o strongly agreed.

41.1% (7) agreed.

41.1% (7) expressed no strong opinion.

17.6% (3) disagreed.

o strongly disagreed.

o returned that contribution to, and line management by, the Reducing Re-Offending group is one of the most significant components of the Managing Chaplain's job description.

29.4% (5) returned that contribution to, and line management by, the Reducing Re-Offending group is one of the least significant components of the Managing Chaplain's job description.

11. The current Managing Chaplain should ensure equality of religious provision for all faiths.

52.9% (9) strongly agreed.

41.1% 97) agreed.

5.8% (1) expressed no strong opinion.

o disagreed.

o strongly disagreed.

23.5% (4) expressed that ensuring the equality of religious provision for all faiths is one of the Managing Chaplain's most important duties.

o expressed the view that ensuring the equality of religious provision for all faiths is one of the Managing Chaplain's least important duties.

12. The current Managing Chaplain should lead Christian courses.

11.7% (2) strongly agreed.

58.8% (10) agreed.

29.4% (5) expressed no strong opinion.

0 disagreed.

0 strongly disagreed.

11.7% (2) respondents indicated that the leading of Christian courses by the Managing Chaplain is one his most important duties.

11.7% (2) respondents indicated that the leading of Christian courses by the Managing Chaplain is one of his least important duties.

Findings from Senior Management Team

The SMT at Haverigg Prison is made up of eleven personnel, not including the Managing Chaplain. Each member received the same survey questionnaire and participation consent form as the randomly selected general prison staff above. Two completed returns (representing the views of 18.1% of the SMT) were received as follows:

1. The Managing Chaplain at Haverigg Prison should be a member of the Senior Management Team.

9% (1) strongly agreed.

0 agreed.

9% (1) expressed no strong opinion.

0 disagreed.

0 strongly disagreed.

0 viewed membership of the SMT as one of the most important tasks of the Managing Chaplain.

0 viewed membership of the SMT. as one of the least important tasks of the Managing Chaplain.

2. The current Managing Chaplain should conduct and lead services of Christian worship.

0 strongly agreed.

18.1% (2) agreed.

0 expressed no strong opinion.

0 disagreed.

0 strongly disagreed.

9% (1) expressed a view that the conducting and leading of Christian worship are among the most important tasks of the Managing Chaplain.

0 returned an opinion that the leading and conducting of Christian worship are among the least important tasks of the Managing Chaplain.

3. The current Managing Chaplain should co-ordinate and organize worship for non-Christians.

0 Strongly agreed.

9% (1) agreed.

9% (1) expressed no strong opinion.

0 disagreed.

0 strongly disagreed.

0 responded that, in their opinion, the co-ordinating and organizing of worship for non-Christians is among the most important of the Managing Chaplain's duties.

9% (1) regarded the co-ordinating and organizing of worship for non-Christians as among the least important duties of the Managing Chaplain.

4. The current Managing Chaplain should make Jesus known to all.

0% strongly agreed.

9% (1) agreed.

0 expressed no strong opinion.

0 disagreed.

0 strongly disagreed.

9% (1) did not tick any of the available boxes.

9% (1) expressed the view that making Jesus known to all is among the most important of the Managing Chaplain's tasks.

0 responded that making Jesus known to all is among the least important of the Managing Chaplain's tasks.

5. The current Managing Chaplain should be invited to (and attend) key operational and policy meetings within the prison.

9% (1) strongly agreed.

9% (1) agreed.

0 expressed no strong opinion.

0 disagreed.

0 strongly disagreed.

0 viewed the invitation and attendance at key operational and policy meetings among the most important of the Managing Chaplain's tasks.

o viewed the invitation and attendance at key operational and policy meetings among the least important of the Managing Chaplain's tasks.

6. The current Managing Chaplain should seek to make Christian disciples.

o strongly agreed.

o agreed.

18.1% (2) expressed no strong opinion.

o disagreed.

o strongly disagreed.

o responded that one of the Managing Chaplain's most important tasks is to seek to make disciples.

o responded that one of the Managing Chaplain's least important tasks is to seek to make disciples.

7. The current Managing Chaplain should proactively represent the prison favorably to the public.

9% (1) strongly agreed.

9% (1) agreed.

o expressed no strong opinion.

o disagreed.

o strongly disagreed.

o returned that proactively representing the prison favorably to the public is one of the Managing Chaplain's most important tasks.

9% (1) returned that proactively representing the prison favorably to the public is one of the Managing Chaplain's least important tasks.

8. The current Managing Chaplain should champion non-Christian faith interests.

9% (1) strongly agreed.

0 agreed.

0 expressed no strong opinion.

9% (1) disagreed.

0 strongly disagreed.

0 viewed the championing of non-Christian faith interests as one of the most important duties of the Managing Chaplain.

9% (1) viewed the championing of non-Christian faith interests as one of the least important duties of the Managing Chaplain.

9. The current Managing Chaplain should promote all faiths.

0 strongly agreed.

9% (1) agreed.

0 expressed no strong opinion.

9% (1) disagreed.

0 strongly disagreed.

0 expressed the view that the promotion of all faiths by the Managing Chaplain is one of his most important tasks.

0 expressed the view that the promotion of all faiths by the Managing Chaplain is one of his least important tasks.

10. The current Managing Chaplain should contribute to, and be line-managed by, the Reducing Re-Offending group.

0 strongly agreed.

9% (1) agreed.

0 expressed no strong opinion.

9% (1) disagreed.

0 strongly disagreed.

0 returned that contribution to, and line management by, the Reducing Re-Offending group is one of the most significant components of the Managing Chaplain's job description.

9% (1) returned that contribution to, and line management by, the Reducing Re-Offending group is one of the least significant components of the Managing Chaplain's job description.

11. The current Managing Chaplain should ensure equality of religious provision for all faiths.

9% (1) strongly agreed.

9% (1) agreed.

0 expressed no strong opinion.

0 disagreed.

0 strongly disagreed.

9% (1) expressed the view that ensuring the equality of religious provision for all faiths is one of the Managing Chaplain's most important duties.

0 expressed the view that ensuring the equality of religious provision for all faiths is one of the Managing Chaplain's least important duties.

12. The current Managing Chaplain should lead Christian courses.

0 strongly agreed.

9% (1) agreed.

0 expressed no strong opinion.

0 disagreed.

0 strongly disagreed.

9% (1) did not tick any of the available boxes.

0 respondents indicated that the leading of Christian courses by the Managing Chaplain is one his most important duties.

0 respondents indicated that the leading of Christian courses by the Managing Chaplain is one of his least important duties.

Analysis of Findings

The intention of the survey was to ascertain not what the Managing Chaplain does or does not do, but the *perception* of what the Managing Chaplain should, or should not do, in the opinion of the general prison staff, employed and contracted. In addition, the same set of questions was sent out to each member of the SMT. Together the returns should have produced a "snapshot of perception" weighted toward the leaders and local policy makers of the prison. However, soon after distribution to the SMT, one of the most senior and influential members told me, quite emphatically, that they did not like the survey and would not be completing it. Two surveys had been returned before these comments were made to me—and none returned after. There is a possibility that, the influential person having made their views known, that the other members of the SMT may have felt that returning theirs would be viewed as an act of disloyalty. Therefore, while figures were collated, and some analysis drawn from them below, it is not felt that they carry enough significance to conclude an accurate perception of the role of the Chaplain from an SMT perspective.

Behind each statement lies a rationale, which falls into one of three areas;

1. To do with pure management issues.

2. To do with predominantly Christian issues.

3. To do with minority faiths.

Each statement, and the results of the returns, are analyzed below;

1. The Managing Chaplain at Haverigg Prison should be a member of the Senior Management Team.

The rationale behind this statement is to do with pure management. It questions the legitimacy of Chaplains sitting on the highest decision-and-local-policy-making body in the prison. Prior to "Fair and Sustainable" the Governing Governor of each prison made their own decision as to which personnel sat on the SMT. Some management teams were quite large and included the Co-ordinating Chaplain, while others were relatively minimal, and did not include the Co-ordinating Chaplain. Chaplains themselves were divided as to whether it was beneficial, or not, to be part of the SMT. Two schools of thought among Chaplains held legitimate validity. Those who believed it was not beneficial did so because they viewed it as a challenge to the independence and neutrality that Todd and Tipton had observed as a quality in 2011.[1] Indeed, they may have viewed membership of the SMT as lining up with Hobhouse's observation in 1922 that "chaplains are . . . far too deeply involved in officialdom . . . that their Christian work is hampered."[2] Those who saw advantages in being selected for membership of the SMT identified that they were being offered a valuable voice with which to speak into the important issues of the day. It brought them back, in their view, to at least somewhere near the status they had enjoyed when the 1877 Prison Rule described Chaplains as co- "superior officers of the prison."

The current perception in Haverigg is equally polarized. Over half of the respondents take the view that chaplaincy membership on the SMT is a good thing, and indeed is one of the most important of the Managing Chaplain's tasks. This, coming from the returns from the general prison staff, suggests that they are

1. Todd and Tipton, *Multi-Faith Prison Chaplaincy*, 5.
2. Hobhouse and Brockway, English *Prisons Today*, 188.

comfortable with the Chaplain holding a management position, and that it is not a threat to impartiality. However, the considerably smaller group of those who expressed that the Chaplain should not be a part of the SMT make-up, also indicated that membership was one of the least important of the Chaplain's tasks. Added to this is that a significant number of those who expressed no strong opinion regarding SMT membership, still felt that it should be one of the least important considerations. Those in this group represent over a third of respondents.

As previously indicated, the finding drawn from the current SMT carries little weight, due to the low number of returns. However, of those who did indicate, one person strongly agreed that membership was beneficial and that it was one of the most important of the Chaplain's duties, while the other expressed no strong opinion.

2. The current Managing Chaplain should conduct and lead services of Christian worship.

The rationale behind this statement is to do with the predominantly Christian practice of conducting and leading services. The current Managing Chaplain is licensed by the Bishop of Carlisle to the "cure of souls" and to specifically use only those forms of service authorized for use in Anglican churches. However, the practice at Haverigg is that not all acts of worship are specifically Anglican. The main corporate service held on a Sunday morning is shown in the chaplaincy printed program as "C.of E./Free Church Communion." Thus, this service could legitimately be led by another ordained minister. The survey returns show that the understanding of all staff is that they agree or strongly agree that the current Managing Chaplain should conduct and lead services. In addition, over one-third indicated that this is one of the Managing Chaplain's most important tasks. An anomaly is that, although all agreed in one form or another with the statement, two respondents saw the leading and conducting of services as one of the Managing Chaplain's least important tasks.

Acknowledging limited credibility due to the small number of returns from the SMT, both managers who chose to respond agreed with the statement. One returned an opinion that it was one of the Managing Chaplain's most important duties, while the other expressed it to be one of the least important.

3. The current Managing Chaplain should co-ordinate and organize worship for non-Christians.

The rationale behind this statement is linked with the multi-faith nature of prison chaplaincy, and the part that a Christian leader should have in the facilitation of those faith practices with which there are fundamental theological differences. It seeks to probe the concept of pluralism and the acceptability of the Christian view of the uniqueness of Christ. The plurality referred to here is specifically "religious," as opposed to "cultural" plurality. Newbigin helpfully distinguishes between cultural and religious plurality when he identifies the simple fact that people of different cultural and religious background, nationality, and languages live peaceably together in our towns and cities (and prisons). This "cultural plurality" can be an enrichment to human life. It is, however, markedly different from "religious pluralism," which holds that:

> The differences between the religions are not a matter of truth and falsehood, but of different perceptions of one truth; that to speak of religious beliefs as true or false is inadmissable. Religious belief is a private matter. Each of us is entitled to have—as we say—a faith of our own. This is religious pluralism.[3]

The responses to the survey, from both the general staff population and the managers of the prison, suggest that over half of the staff at Haverigg understand that, although the Managing Chaplain is an ordained Christian, he has a significant role in upholding the religious plurality described by Newbigin.

3. Newbigin, *Pluralist Society*, 14.

4. The current Managing Chaplain should make Jesus known to all.

The rationale behind this statement is concerned with the predominantly Christian issue of evangelism. At the Chaplain's installation service the Diocesan Bishop asks the priest a series of questions to which the answer must be positive. One of these installation questions from the Bishop to the Chaplain is "will you make Jesus known to all those in your care?" Writing in the journal, "Faith Initiative Embracing Diversity," the author of this dissertation explains how the potential tensions in leading a multi-cultural, inter-faith Chaplaincy Team can be addressed. The balance can be held, it is argued, by seeing the role of the Chaplaincy Team leader as "both a job and a ministry."[4] The returns from the survey suggest, however, that Haverigg Prison staff do not share the view that bringing Jesus to the attention of all is central to the Managing Chaplain's role. Most respondents who expressed a view disagreed, at some level, with the statement "the current Managing Chaplain should make Jesus known to all." This suggests an implicit agreement with Newbigin's description (within the context of describing religious pluralism) that "religious belief is a private matter."[5] Almost half of the respondents expressed no strong opinion. It may be that, at the time of writing, there were heightened sensitivities concerning faith issues in Haverigg, and indeed across the Prison Service as a whole. These are positive sensitivities arising from greater knowledge following the introduction of mandatory staff faith-awareness training—positive in terms of showing respect to all faiths and none, as opposed to being reluctant to comment on faith issues due to being afraid of offending one faith group or another.

4. Jones, *More than Just a Statement*, 32-3.

5. Newbigin, *Pluralist Society*, 14.

5. The current Managing Chaplain should be invited to (and attend) key operational and policy meetings within the prison.

The rationale behind this statement is clearly to do with purely management issues. However, it also has to do with models of Christian church leadership style and practice. The current debate in Christian circles appears to fluctuate between those who emphasize the pastoral nature of Christian leadership, often citing the shepherd motif as an example, and those who favor the management, or CEO, style of leadership. As has already been observed, John Piper emphatically calls upon Christian leaders to reject worldly models, while Andy Stanley takes a high view of secular style leadership.

The statement that participants were asked to comment on should disclose which model is perceived to be the most appropriate for Haverigg at this time. Overwhelmingly, every respondent agreed or strongly agreed that the current Managing Chaplain should be invited to (and attend) key operational and policy meetings within the prison. While this does not reflect negatively on more pastoral models, it does indicate a strong perception of the Managing Chaplain being seated among the local decision-and-policy makers in very much a management-oriented role.

6. The current Managing Chaplain should seek to make Christian disciples.

The rationale behind this statement is to do with the Christian concept of mission—specifically, the understanding of the Great Commission in Matthew's gospel, whereby Christians are commanded to "go and make disciples." The range of literature concerning the Christian mission is widespread; for this dissertation, three significant monographs have been examined in depth, due to their relevance to Christian mission and Christian leadership.

John Stott's is the earliest relevant evaluation of mission.[6] His chosen methodology is based around words and their meanings. He explains his own rationale for this and acknowledges that time changes the meanings of words by quoting C.S.Lewis in one of his "Letters to Malcolm," in which Lewis wrote: "The idea of 'timeless English' is sheer nonsense. No living language can be timeless. You might as well ask for a motionless river."[7] The terminology for "Chaplain" has similarly changed over the years. The current term, as previously explained, has developed into "Managing Chaplain." Stott examines his theme under five broad headings, namely, mission, evangelism, dialogue, salvation, and conversion. All of these areas are relevant to the role of the Managing Chaplain. Stott's method is to study these words, not in isolation from proclamation and action, but as part of a "holistic understanding," which he describes elsewhere as, ". . . a comprehensive activity which embraces evangelism and social action and refuses to let them be divorced."[8] One of the reasons for including a statement about making disciples is to ascertain whether the staff at Haverigg understands the mutual necessity of management (social action) and evangelism in the way that Stott describes.

David Bosch reviews mission in its entirety to show how, historically, a number of paradigms have influenced the Christian understanding of salvation and mission. The strength of opinion among those who disagreed with the statement that the current Managing Chaplain should seek to make Christian disciples may indicate that a proportion agree with Bosch when he argues that "mission is not primarily an activity of the church, but an attribute of God."[9] Alternatively, they may have made a simple link between the making of disciples and proselytizing.

The third literary contribution to this area is the most recent, Christopher Wright's, "The Mission of God."[10] Within the context

---

6. Stott, *Christian Mission*

7. Ibid.

8. Stott, *The Contemporary Christian*, 337.

9. Bosch, *Transforming Mission*, 10.

10. Wright, *The Mission of God.*

of the survey statement the underlying questions are "Whose mission is it?" Does it belong to the Chaplain, or the Christian community? Does it indeed have a place at all within the concentrated multi-faith environment of a prison?" Wright strongly questions the validity of defining mission in a way that overemphasizes the efforts of mankind. He argues for the priority of *God's* mission. In reinforcement of the *Missio Dei*, Wright deconstructs words traditionally related to mission to give a broader, more complete understanding and definition. Other contributors to the "mission debate" include David Hesselgrave and Ed Stetzer,[11] A.J. Kostenberger,[12] and Lesslie Newbigin.[13] With the weight of such credible theologians still debating the nature and definition of mission it is, perhaps, of little surprise that the majority of respondents indicated that they had no strong opinion on this matter.

7. The current Managing Chaplain should proactively represent the prison favorably to the public.

The rationale behind this statement is to do with pure management issues. What is the managerial balance between the Managing Chaplain promoting a high image of the prison and MOJ policies, and of being a "critical friend" who challenges the ethos of national and local policies? On one extreme the Managing Chaplain would, in a protectionist manner, give assent to *all* policies and actively promote them favorably to the public, regardless of the ethical implications. The opposite extreme is taking a stance outside the confines and confidentiality of the SMT and publicly (to some degree) exposing wrongdoing. The Co-ordinating Chaplain from 2007 has notes from a policy at Haverigg that he perceived as so improper that he submitted his resignation. More significantly, in terms of the survey statement, the notes show that, in distancing himself from the policy, he "went public," in that he reported the matter

11. Hesslegrave and Stetzer, *Missionshift.*
12. Kostenberger, *The Place of Mission.*
13. Newbigin, *Trinitarian Doctrine.*

and his impending resignation to the Diocesan Bishop. Given the development of role from Co-ordinating to Managing Chaplain, the probe behind the statement is: "Would this be a realistic course of action today?"

Almost all of the respondents agreed or strongly agreed that the Managing Chaplain should proactively represent the prison favorably to the public, and a little under a quarter took the view that this is one of the most important tasks of the Managing Chaplain. The strength of this collective opinion gives rise to the view that the role of the Managing Chaplain is very much an integral part of prison management. It displays a high view of the status of the Managing Chaplain as one who is trusted to represent the establishment to the outside world. At Haverigg, the Managing Chaplain is also the Media Liaison Officer, a post directly appointed by the Governing Governor.

8. The current Managing Chaplain should champion non-Christian faith interests.

The rationale behind this statement is to do with support for minority faiths. It seeks to address the question of whether, "if the Managing Chaplain becomes the representational voice and champion of non-Christian faiths, does this inevitably lead to a syncretism of all beliefs." Parshall, in quoting Hendrick Kraemer, defines syncretism as "a systematic attempt to combine, blend and reconcile inharmonious, even often conflicting elements, in a so-called synthesis."[14] With the majority of responses supporting the statement that the current Managing Chaplain should champion non-Christian faith interests, there is an inference that Haverigg staff support a fusion of diverse belief systems. Similar to the responses to the statement that the current Managing Chaplain should make Jesus known to all, nearly half of the respondents expressed no strong opinion. Again, this could indicate a reluctance

14. Parshall, *Muslim Evangelism*, 45.

to potentially offend, or it could equally be born out of an informed position following the staff faith-awareness training.

9. The current Managing Chaplain should promote all faiths.

The rationale behind this statement is to do with minority faiths. Some of the previous statements naturally lead into areas of the proclamation of Christ, religious pluralism, and syncretism. This statement encourages a response beyond the support of non-Christians. Essentially, it endeavors to establish the view of the staff concerning the uniqueness of Christ, and how a Christian Managing Chaplain should display that truth. Newbigin, Kostenberger, and Stott all make contributions to the uniqueness of Christ debate in this context.

In his argument against Berger's "plausibility structure" in "The Heretical Imperative," (in which one is called to be orthodox to modern scientific methods, to which all truth claims must be subject) Newbigin points to the fourth gospel's claim, which he describes as, "massively presented"

> that in the man Jesus there was actually present the one who is the Creator and Sustainer and Lord of the entire universe, that He is the light of the world, and that it is only in that light that both the world religions and the whole structure of modern science will be ultimately seen for what they are.[15]

Kostenberger notes that John (in 1 John) does not exhort his readers to direct dialogue with a world that is caught up with sin and resolutely hardened against Jesus, his followers, and the gospel (1 John 2: 15-17). Indeed, he suggests that John is urging believers to closer union (against those who are in opposition) with a simplicity that recognizes that an unbelieving world stands ultimately against Christ and his own. In terms of recognizing the dangers Kostenberger asserts that this should

---

15. Newbigin, *Foolishness to the Greeks*, 10-18.

warn us against both a complacent accommodation to
the world and undue optimism as we seek to engage it in
terms of the Gospel[16]

In contrast, Stott includes dialogue as a positive aspect, at the
same time charting the dangers of extreme positions at each end of
the spectrum. At one end he takes issue with Martin Lloyd Jones's
view that "God is not to be discussed or debated," and at the other
extreme Professor J.G. Davies, who sees preaching as authoritative,
dogmatic, and arrogant. Stott's middle view is that proclamation of
the gospel must always engage sensitively and relevantly, and at
the same time monologue must not be proud. His opinion is that
dialogue should be entered into openly, without suspending our
convictions or the truth and integrity of the gospel.[17]

The understanding of the relevance of plurality, dialogue, and
engagement to the statement under consideration is vital. While
their methodologies may differ, nevertheless Newbigin, Kostenberger, and Stott appear to reach the same conclusion, that plurality as diverse culture is not a threat to the upholding of Christianity.
However, pluralism expressed as parity between belief systems,
none being superior or inferior to any other, is unrealistic and
unacceptable to *all* religions. The concept that drives *all* three to
this conclusion is a belief that there is, contrary to postmodern
opinion, an "absolute truth" to be known.

The findings show that nearly all of the staff at Haverigg agree
or strongly agree that the current Managing Chaplain should *promote* belief systems that are inharmonious with his own Christian
views. A considerably smaller percentage of respondents agreed
that this was one of the most important of his tasks, while none
returned that they considered it to be one of the least important.
One member of the SMT disagreed with the statement.

16. Kostenberger and O'Brien, *Salvation*, 231.

17. Stott, *Christian Mission*, 88–91.

10. The current Managing Chaplain should contribute to, and be line-managed by, the Reducing Re-Offending group.

The rationale behind this statement is to do with management issues, but also to explore the place within the structure that is perceived to be the most effective for the Managing Chaplain to carry out both his managerial and pastoral functions. A range of opinions was expressed, but none thought that placement within the structure was one of the most important issues. While nearly half agreed with the statement, another group of nearly half of the total expressed no strong opinion. The remainder, including one SMT member, disagreed. The section on the history of the perception of the role of Chaplain shows that there was a time when status within the structure was reflected by key number. The Governing Governor was key set 1, while the Chaplain drew key set 3, and was accountable directly to the Governing Governor. The current Managing Chaplain at Haverigg is key set number 362 and is answerable to, and line-managed by, the Head of Reducing Re-offending, a rank of the same grade (band 7). It is the subject of debate whether this change in position is a reflection, indeed a significant reduction, in the overall status and standing of the Chaplain, or simply a more effective and central place for the work and ministry to operate from.

11. The current Managing Chaplain should ensure equality of religious provision for all faiths.

The rationale behind this statement is to do not only with provision for all faiths, but also to address the concept of inter-faith working. In 1998 James Beckford and Sophie Gilliat conducted an in-depth investigation into "Anglican Brokerage."[18] This work probes the tensions between the Church of England and other faiths represented in the Prison Service. It charts the rise in numbers of prisoners from non-Christian traditions and seeks to expose a struggle for equality due to Anglican Chaplains being primary facilitators

18. Beckford and Gilliat, *Religion in Prison*, 28.

of religious and pastoral provision. Beckford and Gilliat argue that religious ethnic communities are subject to a dependence upon an Anglican gate-keeper of facilities, and that this position of inequality should be reconsidered by the Prison Service. In support of this they quote Prison Standing Order 7A of 1989:

> The Prison Service respects the need for all prisoners to be free to practice their religion. It makes provision, therefore for prisoners to participate in worship and other religious activities of a kind that may lead to personal growth, the fullest possible life in the prison setting and preparation for release into the community at the end of a sentence.

The findings show general staff and managers alike are in overwhelming agreement that the current Managing Chaplain should ensure equality of religion for all faiths. Almost a quarter of returns indicated also that this is one of the most important of the Managing Chaplain's roles. None disagreed in any form, and none believed it to be a least important task. If the perception is derived from what is seen in practice at Haverigg, then this disqualifies the contemporary relevance of Beckford and Gilliat. Their contribution to the current position of true equality may well be seen as one of the major contributing influences to the current situation.

12. The current Managing Chaplain should lead Christian courses.

While the rationale behind this statement is clearly to do with Christian issues, it also has an inclination toward the perception of Christian courses as "interventions." In 2005 Jonathan Burnside et al. published research commissioned by the Prison Service into the effectiveness of faith-based units in prisons.[19] It examined the findings of a detailed investigation into the Kainos faith-based program in the period 2000/1 and their impact upon reconviction rates. It details the roots of faith-based units in South America and

19. Burnside et al., *My Brother's Keeper.*

compares the UK Programme with similar programs in the United States. Burnside makes comparisons between those interventions that are successful and those that are not. The conclusion appears to be that faith-based units can and do reduce re-offending, as well as making prisons and punishment more humane.

After developing this earlier research, Burnside delivered a lecture at the European Conference of the International Prison Chaplaincy Association, on May 28 in Springe, Germany. This was subsequently written up verbatim and published in *Justice Reflections* as an article dedicated solely to examining religious interventions in prisons.[20] After introducing his subject with the acknowledgment that religious interventions in prisons are becomingly increasingly important, Burnside goes on to give his top observations, under ten separate headings, summarized as follows:

1. They offer prisons and correctional services something unique:[21] Burnside argues that if, as some believe, it is necessary to have an experience of God in order to love and be loved, then religious interventions do indeed have a unique role to play and quotes the "four images" of psychologist Hugo Veronese in support of this claim.

2. They can have broad appeal in prisons:[22] Following his research Burnside believes that many prisoners have a genuine desire for faith. He found that the faith-based units that came under his scrutiny attracted three different types of prisoners:

   a) Those prisoners who genuinely wanted to change their behavior and who saw this religious intervention as an opportunity to do so;

   b) Those who volunteered because they thought it would be an easy option;

20. Burnside, *Religious Interventions.*
21. Ibid., 2.
22. Ibid., 3.

  c) The more religious prisoners, who wanted to be in a faith-centered environment.[23]

3. They are not miracle cures for criminal behavior and things take time.[24] Burnside acknowledges that there is pressure on service-providers to produce almost instant results in order to prove their worth. He points out, however, that seeds take time to root and that the very best of interventions of any kind take time to develop. He illustrates the problem of prisoners coming to terms with living in a community and the divide between the religious intervention and the real world. He concludes this observation with: "Preparing prisoners for what their world is like is an important aspect of religious interventions. Otherwise, it's a bit like turning people out of hospitals in their pyjamas."[25]

4. Religious interventions are not enough and need to be meshed with non-religious prison programs.[26] Burnside argues that there should be no dualism, while acknowledging the unrest that may appear if there is a perception of receiving public funds for the promotion of a purely religious ideology.

5. They show prisoners' capacity for living in a cohesive community: Burnside makes the statement that:

> the easiest community to form in a prison is a negative community and the most difficult community to form is an inclusive community. At their best, faith-based regimes provide an approximation to living in a 'family', often for prisoners lacking any such experience.[27]

Burnside believes that there is an appetite for positive, communal living in prison.

---

23. Ibid., 3–4.
24. Ibid., 5.
25. Ibid., 6.
26. Ibid., 7.
27. Ibid., 8.

6. They show prisoners' capacity for taking on responsibility: Burnside points out that there is a certain irony in making prisoners *retrospectively* responsible for their behavior (the reason we imprison them) and then denying them *prospective* responsibility by taking away most of their responsibility while in custody. He explains it thus:

> We take citizens and turn them into prisoners and then expect them, with minimal preparation to turn back into citizens again, with all the responsibilities this involves for themselves, their families and for others.[28]

7. Create relationships between prisoners and the community: Burnside observes that the experience for prisoners of links with community volunteers is invaluable and confidently asserts that:

> Research into desistance from crime has suggested that sustained desistance is more likely where a prisoner has strong ties to a community and available social supports beyond prison.[29]

8. One of the biggest interventions is contact with free-world volunteers: Burnside points out the strong symbolism of volunteers giving up their time and resources to stand alongside those in the prison community. He draws again on the psychologist Veronese, who he quotes as saying "the State, an impersonal entity, can build prisons, nominate agents, assign resources – but cannot give love. It is only we, physical persons . . . that can face the challenge of seeding love in the prisons."[30] Burnside notes that Veronese's observations are a two-way process. On the one hand, religious interventions show prisoners' capacity to form a cohesive community; by the same token, Burnside observes the following:

28. Ibid., 9.
29. Ibid., 10.
30. Ibid., 11.

9. They also show the community's capacity to volunteer to be part of the community that is being created:[31] Burnside believes that prisons have no idea of the work involved in recruiting suitable volunteers and that prison volunteering is always exposed to the risk of attracting the wrong sort of volunteers. He sees the need to strike a balance between those potential volunteers who have character flaws that may cause damage to the community, and those who have experienced similar pain and troubles as those prisoners who they come alongside and bring a mature empathy to the situation. What is needed, he suggests, is:

> volunteers who have been 'healed enough' to give an honest account of the failures of their lives. Volunteers who haven't healed enough and who are still bleeding from their wounds just bleed all over the inmates and don't help the inmates to recognise that healing can come. What is needed is an example of someone who has been there, done that, and God has healed them so it gives . . . hope.[32]

10. Prisoners are not the biggest problem facing religious interventions[33]: Burnside holds the opinion that the very nature of custodial institutions is to hold power. He believes that prisons necessarily have to be about management and that any intervention program, once established and deemed to be successful, is in danger of being hijacked by the prison authorities and reshaped to present as an entirely different model. In support of this he uses the illustration of the Kairos Christian intervention project, which, he says, was criticized in the United Kingdom not because it aimed to improve the quality of prisoners' lives, but because of its Christian identity and use of volunteers.

31. Ibid., 12.
32. Ibid., 13.
33. Ibid., 14.

It would appear that considerable progress has been made since Burnside's report. Implicitly, when the survey statement asked if the current Managing Chaplain should lead Christian courses, it was examining the staff perception of the religious interventions that Burnside addresses. Nearly three-quarters of respondents agreed or strongly agreed with the statement, with a proportion believing that it is indeed one of the Managing Chaplain's most important tasks. An equal number, however, also returned that they believed that it is one of the least important tasks. It is reasonable to conclude that Haverigg staff believes religious interventions to be a valuable and important function of the Managing Chaplain.

Conclusion

Identifying and grouping the statements into the three areas of management emphasis, Christian emphasis, and minority faith emphasis, the following charts indicate the strength of perception of staff and management in the different areas.

Chart 1. Staff Perception of the Management Emphasis

67.6% agree that the emphasis is on management.

10.2% disagree that the emphasis is on management.

22% expressed no strong opinion.

0.2% chose not to return.

Chart 2. Staff Perception Christian Emphasis

45.5% agree that the emphasis is on Christian issues.

14.7% disagree that the emphasis is on Christian issues.

35% expressed no strong opinion.

4.6% chose not to return.

Chart 3. Staff Perception of the Minority Faith Emphasis

70.5% agree that the emphasis is on minority faiths.

8.8% disagree that the emphasis is on minority faiths.

20.5% expressed no strong opinion.

0.2% chose not to return.

5

PERCEPTION OF THE LEADERSHIP STYLE OF THE MANAGING CHAPLAIN AT HAVERIGG PRISON

EVALUATION OF THE LEADERSHIP style of the Managing Chaplain is in two parts. The first uses a quantitative method and is drawn from those who work collaboratively with the Managing Chaplain. The second part employs a qualitative method from prisoner focus groups.

Findings from the Core Chaplaincy Team

The core Chaplaincy Team comprises ten members. Each received a participation consent form and survey. Participants were asked to respond to twelve statements by ticking a box on a Likert scale. Ten questionnaires were issued and six returned, representing 60% of the total team.

1. The current Managing Chaplain knows what he wants and how to achieve it.

   Strongly agreed: 50% (3)

   Agreed: 33.3% (2)

Expressed no strong opinion: 16.6% (1)

Disagreed: 0

Strongly disagreed: 0

2. The current Managing Chaplain is concerned for people and has their interests at heart—while still achieving the task.

Strongly agreed: 50% (3)

Agreed: 33.3% (2)

Expressed no strong opinion: 16.6% (1)

Disagreed: 0

Strongly disagreed: 0

3. The current Managing Chaplain is able to react to what is needed in times of rapidly changing situations and circumstances.

Strongly agreed: 33.3% (2)

Agreed: 50% (3)

Expressed no strong opinion:16.6% (1)

Disagreed: 0

Strongly disagreed: 0

4. The current Managing Chaplain motivates others by his charisma, personality, and presence.

Strongly agreed: 0

Agreed: 83.3% (5)

Expressed no strong opinion: 16.6% (1)

Disagreed: 0

Strongly disagreed: 0

5. The current Managing Chaplain completes set tasks with competence.

Strongly agreed: 33.3% (2)

Agreed: 50% (3)

Expressed no strong opinion: 16.6% (1)

Disagreed: 0

Strongly disagreed: 0

6. The current Managing Chaplain exercises direct leadership and takes responsibility for others.

Strongly agreed: 66.6% (4)

Agreed: 16.6% (1)

Expressed no strong opinion: 16.6% (1)

Disagreed: 0

Strongly disagreed: 0

7. The current Managing Chaplain is competently able to react to crises and situations as they arise.

Strongly agreed: 66.6% (4)

Agreed: 16.6% (1)

Expressed no strong opinion: 16.6% (1)

Disagreed: 0

Strongly disagreed: 0

8. The current Managing Chaplain is one to whom I would go when in distress.

Strongly agreed: 50% (3)

Agreed: 33.3% (2)

Expressed no strong opinion: 16.6% (1)

Disagreed: 0

Strongly disagreed: 0

9. The current Managing Chaplain exercises intelligent, action-oriented judgment in all situations.

Strongly agreed: 50% (3)

Agreed: 33.3% (2)

Expressed no strong opinion: 16'6% (1)

Disagreed: 0

Strongly disagreed: 0

10. The current Managing Chaplain is able to share decision making in an act of participative leadership.

Strongly agreed: 33.3% (2)

Agreed: 33.3% (2)

Expressed no strong opinion: 16.6% (1)

Disagreed: 0

Strongly disagreed: 0

11. The current Managing Chaplain quickly comprehends issues and needs, and responds appropriately.

Strongly agreed: 50% (3)

Agreed: 33.3% (2)

Expressed no strong opinion: 16.6% (1)

Disagreed: 0

Strongly disagreed: 0

12. The current Managing Chaplain is one to whom I would go when I needed a direct answer.

Strongly agreed: 100% (6)

Agreed: 0

Expressed no strong opinion: 0

Disagreed: 0

Strongly disagreed: 0

Analysis of Findings from the Core Chaplaincy Team

All of the statements under consideration link back into a leadership generation identified by Doyle and Smith in the previous subsection "Overview of Church Leadership Models."[1]

Statements 1, 5, and 9 suggest a trait style of leadership on the Doyle and Smith model. Collectively, 83.3% of respondents indicated that the Managing Chaplain displayed a leaning toward this style of leadership.

Statements 2, 6, and 10 suggest a behavioral style of leadership on the Doyle and Smith model. Collectively again, 83.3% of respondents indicated that the Managing Chaplain showed an inclination toward this style of leadership.

Statements 3, 7, and 11 suggest a contingency style of leadership on the Doyle and Smith model. Yet again, 83.3% of respondents perceived this style in the Managing Chaplain.

---

1. Doyle and Smith, *Born and Bred?*

Statements 4, 8, and 12 suggest a transformational style of leadership on the Doyle and Smith model. Marginally, the returns show a slightly greater emphasis on this style, at 88.3%.

Findings and Analysis from Prisoner Focus Groups

Todd and Tipton identify five prisoner groups who engage with chaplaincy:

1. The devout, who arrive in prison with their own faith tradition, which they wish to continue practicing;

2. The converts, who find faith while in prison;

3. The returners, prisoners who take the opportunity to reconnect to their faith traditions while in custody;

4. The professional seekers, who are generally agnostic and do not subscribe to any particular faith, but will attend a wide range of services and chaplaincy activities;

5. The opportunists, prisoners who openly claim not to be interested in faith or religion but value chaplaincy as a safe space, an escape from the wings.[2]

Mindful of this, four separate prisoner focus groups were established. These were made up from Christians, Muslims, Buddhists, and Sikhs who had agreed to take part and had signed a participation consent form. In each group a question was posed. Following this the researcher simply observed the discussion and made notes of key words and themes as they arose.

The Christian group, made up of nine prisoners, was presented with: "Christianity is a 'missionary religion' that seeks to proclaim the good news of Jesus. The Managing Chaplain at Haverigg happens to be a Christian. What should the balance be between proclaiming the good news . . . and doing good things for all people?" Containing an ordained clergyman among the

2. Todd and Tipton, *Multi-Faith Prison Chaplaincy.*

prisoners, the group was steered by him and his thoughts. They discussed the question in a way that suggested there could be no distinction between proclamation and social action. Specifically, they looked at their own actions within the prison and how they were facilitated to do this by the Managing Chaplain. Negatively, some expression of frustration was made between what they saw as the disproportionate lack of time the Managing Chaplain gives to "his own." Dissent to this general feeling came from a Rastafarian member of the group (who emphatically holds that Rastafarianism is mainstream Christianity). In conclusion, it appeared that the leadership style of the Managing Chaplain allowed and encouraged Christians to worship, but that he spent a disproportionate amount of his time with other faiths.

The Muslim group, made up of five prisoners, was presented with: "How much support do you feel that you have in the practice of your faith in Haverigg Prison?" The conversation swung between a feeling of privilege that they had weekly access to a Muslim cleric who could lead them in prayer, and frustration at not having their own faith leader available at all times, "like the Christians." There appeared to be a consensus that, although they did actually have access to religious items and literature, they had to fight for it. They saw the Managing Chaplain as a good man, but one with whom they had to remain in favor in order to access their own faith.

The Buddhist group, made up of three prisoners, was presented with the same question. The conversation that ensued was remarkably similar to that of the Muslim group. The Buddhists too expressed frustration at having to ask the (Christian) Managing Chaplain for everything, and moreover to plan their own feast and festival arrangements in the absence of a locally available Buddhist leader. They felt that, although their requests for facilities were usually met, the speed with which issues were addressed indicated that Buddhism was a lesser priority.

The same question was put before a Sikh group of two prisoners. This was a very positive conversation, probably due to the recent appointment of a regular (weekly) Sikh minister. The two participants happened to be the total number of Sikh prisoners in Haverigg at that time and, previous to the recent appointment, felt that they had been "looked after by the Chaplain, as far as he could allow." However, they now expressed a strong feeling of "going forward," with direct access to their own faith representative.

Conclusion

Overall, there is a perceived balance between the four identified leadership styles, with the Managing Chaplain being viewed by his peer colleagues as only marginally more into the transformational generation. It might be argued that this is the weakest of the four leadership styles, emphasizing personality over competence. The apparent confidence displayed in the Managing Chaplain should be tempered by the fact the ten participants to whom the survey was sent is made up of eight Christians, one Muslim, and one Sikh. Satisfaction with the Managing Chaplain's style of leadership may well originate from a shared Christian perspective.

The prisoner focus groups, however, suggest that the challenge to "Anglican brokerage" raised as an issue by Beckford and Gilliat in 1998 is still a tension at Haverigg in 2013. Muslim and Buddhist focus groups expressed quite emphatically that they felt a need to do everything through the Anglican gate-keeper. Even the small Sikh group, while acknowledging support from the Christian Managing Chaplain, were relieved to have been appointed their own faith representative, to whom they now had direct access.

6

RECOMMENDATIONS
AND CONCLUSION

THIS WORK HAS SOUGHT, by ethnographic research, to trace the perception of the role of Prison Chaplain in general and, specifically, examine how the current role is practiced at Haverigg Prison.

After contextualizing the setting, geography, and ethos, the first objective summarizes and compares church and secular leadership models. It identifies Doyle and Smith as the most relevant model and subsequently goes on to compare the current Managing Chaplain's leadership style with this model.[1]

The second objective traces the history and development of prison chaplaincy, with particular attention to the perception and status of Chaplains at various points through history—the highest profile of chaplaincy being the 1830 Millbank project, with the combination into one post of Governor and Chaplain, the intention being to draw a close parallel between the reformation of prisoners and religious penitence. The lowest point, however, was arguably 1922, with the scathing Hobhouse/Brockway report that Chaplains were so under the control of the system that their Christian work was "almost fatally flawed."[2]

Employing a mainly quantitative method, the third objective sought to ascertain from Haverigg general staff and management their perception of the role of the current Managing Chaplain. Lack

1. Doyle and Smith, *Born and Bred?*
2. Hobhouse and Brockway, *English Prisons Today.*

of engagement by managers resulted in less weight being given to their views, since only two individuals chose to respond. Analysis of the overall results show that most staff believe that there is an emphasis on management tasks, and that minority faiths take priority over Christian issues.

The final objective was to identify the perception of the leadership style of the current Managing Chaplain, ascertained by a quantitative study of the core Chaplaincy Team, alongside a qualitative study from multi-faith prisoner focus groups. From a chaplaincy staff perspective, the returns indicated a fairly equal balance across all four of Doyle and Smith's generations of leadership styles. It did lean marginally, however, toward the arguably weaker transformational style, emphasizing personality over competence. It was noted that the apparent confidence displayed in the Managing Chaplain should be tempered by the fact the group of ten participants to whom the survey was sent, was made up of eight Christians, one Muslim, and one Sikh. Satisfaction with the Managing Chaplain's style of leadership may well originate from a shared Christian perspective. The outcome from the prisoner focus groups is far less satisfactory. In 1980 Beckford and Gilliat exposed a struggle for equality for minority faiths due to Anglican Chaplains being the primary facilitators of religious and pastoral provision.[3] Acknowledging that Beckford and Gilliat have been major contributors to the redressed balance that the Prison Service currently enjoys, the conclusion drawn from prisoner focus groups is that they are still, at Haverigg, very much dependent upon the Anglican.

With the intention of maintaining the integrity of Christian witness while fully respecting all other faiths, the following measures are recommended:

1. In the light of Tidball's observation to "study the symptoms of an ailing community before issuing the remedy,"[4] bring together all stakeholders (staff, managers, and prisoners from

3. Beckford and Gilliat, *Religion in Prison.*
4. Tidball, *Ministry by the Book.*

all faith groups). The terms of reference for such a meeting would be to identify strengths and weaknesses of current chaplaincy practice at Haverigg.

2. Having studied together the symptoms, an outcome of the above meeting should be a clear action plan.

3. The Managing Chaplain should meet regularly with representatives from individual faith groups in order for there to be a greater mutual understanding of the allocation and stewardship of resources.

BIBLIOGRAPHY

Abbott, W. J. "The Prison Chaplain." *Prison Service Journal* 27, 1968.

Beckford, James A., and Sophie Gilliat. *Religion in Prison: 'Equal Rites' in a Multi-Faith Society*. Cambridge: Cambridge University Press, 1998.

Blom-Cooper, Louis. "'The Penalty of Imprisonment.' The 1987 Tanner Lectures on Human Values." 1987. Accessed July 8, 2013. http://tannerlectures. utah.ed_documents/a-to -z/b/Blom-Cooper88.pdf.

Bosch, David J. *Transforming Mission: Paradigm Shifts in Theology of Mission*. New York: Orbis, 1991.

Burnside, Jonathan, Nancy Loucks, Joanna R. Adler, and Gerry Rose. *My Brother's Keeper. Faith-Based Units in Prisons*. Cullompton: Willan, 2005.

Burnside, Jonathan. "Religious Interventions in Prisons." *Justice Reflections*, 2008.

Carnes, Philip Gene. "Like Sheep Without a Shepherd: The Shepherd Metaphor and its Primacy for Biblical Leadership." Accessed March 24, 2012. http:// virtual.rts.edu/Site/Virtual/Resources/Student_Theses/Carnes-Sheep Without A Shepherd.pdf.

Doyle, Michelle Erina, and Mark K. Smith. *Born and Bred? Leadership, Heart and Informal Education*. London: YMCA, 1999.

Drew, J.H. "The Chaplain's Job Analysis." *Prison Service College,* 1972.

Elkin, Winifred A. *The English Penal System*. Middlesex: Penguin, 1957.

Grudem, Wayne. *Systematic Theology: An Introduction to Biblical Doctrine*. Nottingham: Inter-Varsity, 2007.

Hesselgrave, David J. and Ed. Stetzer. *Missionshift: Global Issues in the Third Millennium*. Nashville: B&H, 2010.

Hobhouse S., and A.F. Brockway, eds. *English Prisons Today: Being the Report of the Prison System Enquiry Committee*. London: Longmans Green, 1922.

Home Office. *Report on the work of the Prison Department 1967*. London: Her Majesty's Stationery Office, 1968.

Jones, Glynn. "More than just a Statement." *Faith Initiative Embracing Diversity* 18, 2007.

Kostenberger, Andreas J., and Peter T. O'Brien. *Salvation to the Ends of the Earth: Biblical Theology of Mission*. Nottingham: Apollos, 2001.

Kostenberger, Andreas J. "The Place of Mission in New Testament Theology: An Attempt to Determine the Significance of Mission Within the Scope of the New Testament's Message as a Whole." Accessed January 13, 2012. http://www.biblicalfoundations.org/pdf/NT%20Theology%20an%20 Mission.PDF.

Merkle, Benjamin L. *The Elder and Overseer: One Office in the Early Church*. New York: Peter Lang, 2003.

Ministry of Justice. "About HM Prison Service." Accessed March 24, 2012. http://www.justice.gov.uk/about/hmps.

———. "Faith and Pastoral Care for Prisoners." *Prison Service Instruction (51/2011)*. Accessed November 22, 2012. http://www.justice.gov.uk/ about/hmps.

National Offender Management Service (NOMS). "NOMS Business Priorities. Fair and Sustainable." *Business Plan 2012-13*: 12-13. Accessed November 22, 2012. http://www.justice.gov.uk/downloads/publications/corporate-reports/noms/2012/noms-business-plan-2012-2013.pdf.

Newbigin, Lesslie. *Foolishness to the Greeks: The Gospel and Western Culture*. Grand Rapids: Eerdmans, 1986.

———. *The Gospel in a Pluralist Society*. London: SPCK, 1989.

———. *The Relevance of Trinitarian Doctrine for Today's Mission*. London: Edinburgh House, 1963.

Noblett, William. "Faith in the Future." *Prison Service News*. 259, 2008.

Parshall, Phil. *New Paths in Muslim Evangelism: Evangelical Approaches to Contextualization*. Grand Rapids: Baker, 1980.

Pearce, Stanley. 1963. "The Chaplain's Place in the Prison Service." *Prison Service Journal*. July 1963.

Piper, John. *Brothers, We Are Not Professionals*. Fearn: Christian Focus, 2008.

Prisons Act 1952. Accessed March 24, 2012. http://www.legislation.gov.uk/ ukpga/Geo6and1Eliz2/15-16/52.

Prison Rules 1999. Accessed March 24, 2012. http://www.legislation.gov.uk/ uksi/1999/728/contents/made.

Prison Service Order 4550 (Religion Manual). Accessed March 24, 2012. http:// www.justice.gov.uk/downloads/.../PSO_4550_religion_manual.doc.

Quinn, Jerome D. and William C. Wacker. *The First and Second Letters to Timothy*. Grand Rapids: *Eerdmans*, 1995.

Rees, Leslie Lloyd. 1972. "The Role of the Chaplain in the Modern World." *Prison Service College*, 1972.

Roman Catholic Prison Chaplains. "Letter to Archbishop Nichols." Accessed July 11, 2013. http://www.thetablet.co.uk/images/Min%20of%20Justice. pdf.

Scott, David. *God's Messengers Behind Bars: A Report Examining the Role and Perception of Christian Prison Chaplains at a Dispersal Prison, a Local*

Prison, a Training Prison, and Two Young Offender Prisons. Edge Hill: Edge Hill University College, 1997.

Stanley, Andy, Marshall Shelley, and Eric Read. "State of the Art." *Leadership Journal.* Spring 2006.

Stott, John. *Christian Mission in the Modern World.* Illinois: Inter-Varsity, 1975.

———. *The Contemporary Christian: An Urgent Plea for Double Listening.* Leicester: Inter-Varsity, 1992.

Tidball, Derek. *Ministry by the Book: New Testament Patterns for Pastoral Leadership.* Nottingham: Apollos, 2008.

Todd, Andrew, and Lee Tipton. *The Role and Contribution of a Multi-Faith Prison Chaplaincy to the Contemporary Prison Service: Final Report.* Cardiff University: Cardiff Centre for Chaplaincy Studies, 2011.

Webb S., and B. Webb. *English Prisons Under Local Government.* London: Longmans, Green, 1922.

Williams, Rowan. "Ministry in Prison: Theological Reflections." *Justice Reflections.* 2003.

Wright, Christopher J.H. *The Mission of God: Unlocking the Bibles Grand Narrative.* Nottingham: Inter-Varsity, 2006.